NAACP IMAGE
AWARD NOMINEE
OUTSTANDING
LITERARY WORK

Sakina Ibrahim, is an NAACP Image Award nominated Author, Performer, Speaker and Youth Empowerment Facilitator. She received her Bachelors of Fine Arts in Dance from the University of the Arts in Philadelphia, PA. She received her Masters of Fine Arts from University of California, Irvine. Her dedication to artistry and education allowed her to receive prestigious grants for her research and work in African Diaspora Dance and Youth Empowerment.

As a scholar Sakina has presented on youth engagement, media, and Black culture at conferences held as University of Albany and California State University and more. She has also served as faculty at Saddleback College, Cypress College, and Westchester Community College, Jill Scott's Blues Babe Foundation and The Dance Theatre of Harlem. Sakina is the former Assistant to legendary Choreographer Donald McKayle and Hollywood Choreographer Anthony Burrell. Sakina's performance credits include *Rennie Harris Rhaw*, Shelly Garrett's *Beauty Shop*, Own Network's *Raising Whitley*, *Bayside the Musical* (Off-broadway) and more. Sakina uses dance, drama, and creative writing to facilitate youth empowerment workshops based on *Big Words to Little Me* with organizations and schools nationally.

Follow us @ facebook.com/bigwordstolittleme

DEDICATION AND ACKNOWLEDGMENTS

Thank you to my Mother Caroline Powell, Grandmothers- Mattie Rosemond, Augusta Wheeler, Luvenia Rosemond, and Atiya Ibrahim. Thank you to my support system and family Auntie Nicki, Uncle Carl, Uncle Darryl, Uncle Gary, My brother Ibin, Jaedyn, Bunmi Samuel and extended friends and family, I love you. Thank you to my mentors and teachers who continue to sow into my life. Thank you to my purpose mates, friends and the incredible support of The Mograbi family, The Panton Family, and the Soka Gakkai International.

This book is dedicated to every young girl in my classes each of you have influenced the vision and need of this book I appreciate and value your life! My gratitude extends beyond imagination... THANK YOU.

"A single flower can completely transform a bleak atmosphere. The important thing, therefore, is to have the spirit, the determination, to improve your environment, to change it for the better, if even just a little." - Daisaku Ikeda

INTRODUCTION
WHO I AM

Hi, I am Sakina, I am a daughter, a sister, a friend, a teacher, a black woman, an artist, the list goes on and on with the many titles I carry for myself. The truth is regardless of all that stuff, I am just like you. I am a girl trying to figure out life the best way I can and become happy. I like who I am. Better yet, I like all of me – my strengths, my success, my looks, my fears, my mistakes - and I embrace all my experiences - my past, my present, and my future. I'm a work in progress and I do my best. I forgive myself when I fall short and I no longer accept less than what is rightfully mine. From the wise words of Toni Morrison, "I do better when I know better."

I am open to the guidance of others but I am no longer defined by it. I surround myself with people whom I admire, adore, trust and respect and I've let go of those who can't see me for the real me. I still get mad, sad and scared but I am also happy, confident and hopeful. My life hasn't been easy. My road has been windy and I definitely walk in crooked lines - but it's my road nevertheless - so I keep moving forward to the best of my ability.

I DIDN'T ALWAYS FEEL THIS WAY...NOT AT ALL! When I was younger, I felt nothing but scared, alone, embarrassed and lost. My dad was in prison, my friends had turned on me, I was tired of acting like an adult when I was just a kid and when I looked around at my life, I didn't like it. I didn't see a future I thought was worth living.

Today, I do. Today, I know different. If only I knew back then what I know now. Back then, I hurt because others hurt me. I was a child in an adult world without the skills to handle it. No one told me what I needed to know. Or, I didn't hear it if they did. I was suffering and no one seemed to care. I was wrong. People did care - maybe not in the ways I wanted or needed or thought they should, but they did. I wasn't looking in the right places or for the right things. I didn't have the information I do now.

TODAY, I LIVE MY LIFE RATHER THAN SIMPLY SURVIVING IT.

Do I still get hurt, yes! Do others hurt me, yes! Do I hurt others, yes! We all get hurt. It's an inescapable part of life. The difference is I've learned how to handle it.

So no matter what your life looks like right now, don't give up. No matter how sad, or scared, or angry you are, it'll be okay. No matter who loves you, who hurts you, or who you need, or who you don't, just hold on. You're in the beginning of your journey and so am I. I'm hoping what I do know might help you. Looking back, I wish BIG ME could have told LITTLE ME what was to come so I wouldn't have worried so much. That's why I'm writing this book - for you. I'm hoping my BIG ME can guide your LITTLE YOU as you become the BIG YOU you are meant to be.

MAY YOUR JOURNEY BE FULL OF GROWTH AND FORWARD MOVEMENT.

CHAPTER ONE
FEELING ALONE / ME TOO

LITTLE ME wanted to fit in but I never felt like I belonged. People whom I thought understood me only disappointed me. Girls gossiped about me, boys frustrated me, school confused me and my family ignored me. I didn't know what I was doing wrong, only that something wasn't right. I knew I was different but I didn't know what was different about me. I felt like a teddy bear left behind on the bus. I, too, was lost and alone.

WE ARE SURROUNDED BY LOVE EVEN WHEN IT IS QUIET AND INVISIBLE.

I thought if I knew what was wrong with me, I could try and fix it. That's why I started comparing myself to others – I wanted to see what they had and I didn't or what I had and they didn't. The problem was that the only information I had to work with was my insides versus their outsides. What I failed to recognize was that the two aren't comparable; feelings and appearances aren't the same. Yet, I made the connection anyways. I assigned feelings based solely on someone's looks and then compared those against how I felt.

For example, when I saw girls smiling, I told myself they had it made in ways I never would. When I noticed girls wearing new outfits, I believed they had a confidence I could never find. When I felt like a misfit, I witnessed other girls hanging out and none of them seemed worried about whether or not they fit in. For whatever reason, I believed everyone felt the exact opposite of what I felt but I never bothered to confirm whether or not my assumptions were even true; they felt right and so they seemed right.

DO YOU COMPARE YOURSELF TO OTHERS AND BELIEVE THEY HAVE IT MADE AND YOU DON'T?

How could I know if those girls had it made, felt confident or worried about fitting in? I couldn't and I didn't yet I acted like I did. I created my own version of their lives even though I didn't have the insight to properly do so. It wasn't fair of me to make such judgments. Basically, what I was doing was incorrectly assigning feelings to others, convincing myself they were true and then proceeding to create a false starting point from which I judged me and everyone else. My search for answers failed. I couldn't fix myself when all I was doing was finding more fault. In fact, I felt more alone and alienated then when I first started.

How could I know if those girls had it made, felt confident or worried about fitting in? I couldn't and I didn't yet I acted like I did. I created my own version of their lives even though I didn't have the insight to properly do so. It wasn't fair of me to make such judgments. Basically, what I was doing was incorrectly assigning feelings to others, convincing myself they were true and then proceeding to create a false starting point from which I judged me and everyone else. My search for answers failed. I couldn't fix myself when all I was doing was finding more fault. In fact, I felt more alone and alienated then when I first started.

WHEN YOU COMPARE, YOU DESPAIR. THE GIRLS WHO SEEM TO HAVE IT ALL ARE SOMETIMES THE GIRLS CARRYING THE MOST PAIN. UNTIL YOU KNOW SOMEONE'S STORY, IT'S UNFAIR TO JUDGE THEM BASED SOLELY ON THEIR APPEARANCE. THINK ABOUT IT – YOU HIDE YOUR OWN PAIN SO OTHERS ARE MORE THAN LIKELY HIDING THEIR OWN PAIN AS WELL.

Similarly, having the information didn't work either. For instance, when I was younger I was told that I was too sensitive. I tried to be less sensitive but I didn't know how to rid myself of my feelings; thick skin doesn't come easy when feelings run deep. In fact, it was awkward. It was like putting a cat suit on a dog and expecting the dog to like it – it wasn't going to happen.

It was hard hiding my feelings because it was unnatural and not in my nature to do so. If it were about fixing a behavior that was hurtful or unnecessary, that would be one thing. But it wasn't. It was about pleasing someone else at my expense. In other words, it wasn't something I needed to change.

Even when I did pull it off, I felt like a fraud because I was withholding pieces of me that I didn't need to be. Turned out, it was important and valuable information for me to have. It taught me to recognize when change is for the right reasons versus the wrong ones. If I change a part of myself and it feels good, then I made a change in the right direction but, if I feel like a fraud or a fake, then I am probably changing something that doesn't need changing. I'm not suggesting change won't feel uncomfortable because it will and it does. What I'm trying to say is changing isn't about hiding who I am but improving. Improving myself, however, is about loving myself more and has nothing to do with accepting myself less.

I don't need to change just because someone tells me I should. Changing myself to please another only robs me of who I truly am. If I allow others to define me, then I am granting them permission to alter my true nature. That's exactly what would have happened if I changed how sensitive I was because my passion and compassion are gifts, not faults. What I needed was self-acceptance and not self-adjustment.

Imagine changing every time a new person criticized you or every time you felt defective? I would be changing every other day, backwards and forwards, this way and that way, until I would be unable to recognize myself anymore.

Feeling a part of isn't about conforming, it's about accepting one another for the similarities that brought you together and celebrating the differences that make everyone unique. Acceptance of others starts with self-acceptance. Those who love themselves love others, while those who dislike themselves, criticize others.

NOTE YOUR OWN BEHAVIOR AND THAT OF THOSE AROUND YOU – ARE YOU CONSTANTLY GOSSIPING ABOUT OTHERS IN ORDER TO MAKE YOURSELF FEEL BETTER? OR ARE YOU CELEBRATING EACH OTHER AND SPREADING LOVE AND GOOD CHEER?

LITTLE ME felt alone and different because I was looking outside of myself to change the feelings that were inside of me. I wanted to be liked and accepted without first liking and accepting myself. I wanted to fix the pieces of me that were broken, damaged or defective but I couldn't because I wasn't broken, damaged or defective – only my perception was. Criticism strips me of my gifts while acceptance honors and encourages me to shine. When I put others down it's because I'm trying to make myself feel better. The same holds true for those who criticize me – they don't accept themselves either and are trying to make themselves feel better by putting me down. Misery loves company and love breeds more love.

Write down 1 thing you would like to change about yourself. Is it because it bothers you or because you think people would like you better?

_____

_____

LITTLE ME was confused, too, when people wanted to bring me down rather than help me rise. I didn't understand why my worst qualities were celebrated while my best traits were ridiculed. Or even more so, when I was accused of believing that I was better than everyone else when all I wanted was a better life than what I had. People laughed at me for having dreams and discouraged me from trying to make them happen. Why? It started to feel like no matter what I did it would never be right. If I tried to dress right, do my hair right, act right and say the right things somehow it just wasn't right. When I skipped school, lied to my mom and hung out with the boys, it didn't sit right. If doing right wasn't right and doing wrong wasn't right, then what was right? The answer was the same – self-acceptance. I wasn't accepted for who I was because I didn't accept myself. At the same time, the ones who couldn't accept me didn't accept themselves, either. I had to learn to love myself before everything else could fall into place.

FIND YOUR PASSION AND YOU WILL FIND YOUR TIME WELL SPENT.

Through all my turmoil, I didn't have anyone to talk to or know how to talk about it even if I did. It was easier to hide and stay silent than open up and face public humiliation. Sliding through unnoticed was preferable even though being alone was the exact thing I was trying to prevent. I focused on the negative and ignored the positive and complained about what I didn't have rather than appreciate what I did. I wanted to change for the wrong reasons and tried too hard. All I knew was that I couldn't get my unhappy feelings to go away no matter what I did. I was a mess.

Write down 3 things you love about yourself.

1. _____

2. _____

3. _____

WHAT LITTLE ME DIDN'T KNOW
I'M NOT ALONE

WHAT BIG ME KNOWS NOW
OTHERS GET ME

HOW I GOT THERE
I STOPPED COMPARING & STARTED SHARING

The truth was that I wasn't alone. I wasn't different, I was not a freak and I was not who people accused me of being. I had insecurities, fears and uncomfortable feelings just like everyone else. Mine might have been more pronounced because I focused so intently on them but not because I was the only one who had them. In fact, other girls worried about how they looked, if they were liked and whether or not they fit in. I wasn't the only girl crying herself to sleep and I wasn't the only one who had big dreams. Nor was I the only girl with a struggling family or the only family facing troubles. I was an insecure girl, lost and confused, trying to find my way. I wasn't alone; it only felt that way. I wasn't different; I only believed that to be true. I had no idea how many girls were out there who totally got me. I had no idea how alike I was when I only knew how different I felt.

Believe in your greatness and your greatness will find you.

In fact, there are girls everywhere who understood who I was, how I felt, and what I thought. My problem wasn't that I was alone but that I kept comparing myself to others without knowing what I was comparing myself against. I was unfairly judging everyone. I denied myself the positive image I deserved and I dismissed other girls as not having pain like mine.

Rather than focusing on myself, I should have been spending my time getting to know others. If I had listened more, I would have heard other girls sharing the same things I was too afraid to share. When I did, I finally heard the two words that changed my life - "me too!" Those simple words made all the difference in the world to me. "Me too!" meant that somebody else understood. "Me too!" meant that I wasn't alone. "Me too!" meant that I wasn't different. The relief I felt knowing someone else had the same problems, the same issues, the same feelings and the same thoughts I did was huge. It was only then that I finally gave up the belief that I was different and defective. By doing so, I gave myself the right to find the self-love and self-acceptance I deserved. It was the beginning of my journey toward loving myself.

So no matter what your situation is and no matter how you feel, you are never alone and you are going to make it! I did. BIG ME found a confidence LITTLE ME never had because I learned to accept myself under any circumstance and amongst any crowd.

I finally learned that I never had to feel alone again and I could celebrate my differences rather than bash myself because of them. The human race is not a species of mismatched beings but is a race of like creatures. We separate ourselves unnecessarily when it is kinder to be united. BIG ME chooses to live my life rather than cower from it.

We all have the right to look fantastic, be confident, appreciate our gifts and love ourselves as we live our lives. The power is within each and every one of us if we are willing to tap into it. All love begins with self-love. I hope you read on and can identify with the pains I struggled with and the solutions I found to them because, all in all, attitude and behavior are a choice – my choice. It's all about figuring out what choices to make.

Find 3 women with whom you would consider sharing your thoughts and feelings. Write their names here.

1. _____

2. _____

3. _____

Listen to the conversations around you and write down if you hear another girl sharing about feelings you experience. Include the date, the person and the feeling shared.

_____

_____

_____

_____

Write about a dream you have and what steps it would take to get there. Don't be afraid to dream as big as you want.

_____

_____

_____

_____

It is our responsibility to treat ourselves right and teach others how to treat us. Sometimes we become a victim to our surroundings and we are unable to change the circumstances that we are in. We sometimes blame ourselves for choices we didn't make. Some things are simply not our fault.

CHAPTER TWO
IT'S NOT YOUR FAULT / THE POWER WITHIN

I grew up in a black and brown neighborhood until I was twelve years old, at which point my uncle was beaten by a gang member, and we moved to the suburbs. I was exposed to circumstances that were beyond my control. Addiction, violence and poverty hit home in ways that many will never understand. A different mentality stems from living in disenfranchised neighborhoods and it affected the way I saw and related to the world. Don't get me wrong – no neighborhood is absent from painful and abusive experiences – but some neighborhoods experience difficulties others don't.

The world isn't fair or equal. I am a black woman. I know. I grew up in a system that was designed for me and not by me. However, people are more similar than different and whether you experience unhappy situations in your home, in your community or in your school, you are not alone, but you are, indeed, affected by it. Everyone is.

We come from a long line of survivors; the blood that runs through our veins has always overcome.

So what happens when the people trusted to care for you, fail you? What are you supposed to do when you are a kid expected to be an adult and the adults are acting like kids? My neighborhood was filled with adults making poor decisions because they lacked the resources required to make better ones. Financial insecurity triggered stress; alcoholism and drug addiction caused problems while living a life of crime wreaked havoc on the family unit. Drugs ran the streets; violence filled the homes. My neighborhood was too tired and too unhappy to change their ways. The mistreatment and enslavement of our ancestors still affected our community.

It wasn't my ancestors' fault they were abused. It wasn't their fault they were forced into poverty and denied rights. They did the best they could and fought for their lives when no one else stood behind them. My ancestors had reasons to blame and reasons to hate. However, because of their courage, times have changed and times are different. I have opportunities they never had and luxuries they weren't afforded. My ancestors didn't teach hate, in fact, they taught me how to fight oppression and stand up for myself. I could continue their forward movement and create a life they weren't permitted or I could keep the cycle of drugs, violence and abuse going. Most of the neighborhood chose the latter and it served only to hold them back.

Learn your ancestry. Find out what was endured, survived and fought to change. The world is still unfair and there are Systems that continue to support racism. Move forward and become the change your community, friends and/or family needs.

My parents brought me into this world safely and for that I am grateful.

My parents made choices in their teens that changed their lives. My mother became a parent and my dad went to prison. She was only eighteen when she gave birth to me. She had to skip the time of her life intended for transitioning into adulthood to raise me. She did an incredible job raising my brother and I but as a teen mom she had to make sacrifices. My mom taught me early on that falling in love and having a baby would not bring happiness or freedom, but instead would bring responsibility for another life and many challenges.

If I follow what went before me, I should expect the same results.

Watching my mother work so hard, for some reason made me feel guilty. Instead of having fun, following her dreams and building friendships, she worked and raised us. I admire her strength for doing what needed to be done, but I sure knew it must of been hard.

Before she had the chance to find herself, she was forced to give up pieces of her life; she put aside her goals and dreams for the sake of her children. Teens aren't ready to be parents because they have life lessons that still need to be learned.

I also grew up feeling unwanted and unloved by my father because he wasn't around. I thought it was my fault but it wasn't; he was incarcerated. Somehow I convinced myself it had something to do with me. I was ashamed of him and I carried this shame all of the time. It was embarrassing every time someone asked about his whereabouts. I didn't know what to tell people. Did I lie or say he was in prison? I had no clue because nobody told me what to say or gave me an alternative answer. No answer would have mattered anyways because the only thing that did matter to me was that he wasn't there.

I had to learn that my father's prison sentence was not a personal reflection about me; it was the result of his own choices. The negative feelings I attached to myself weren't mine to hold. I didn't do it, I didn't cause it, I couldn't fix it and it wasn't my job to change it. Still, it affected me and it took a long time to find the truth.

Describe a choice YOU made that caused you and someone else a problem that was your fault. What could you do to change the situation?

_____

_____

_____

_____

Describe a choice someone else made that caused you a problem that wasn't your fault. How did you handle it?

_____

_____

_____

_____

I had the right to be loved and protected and you have that same right, too. Everything that goes on around me is not a direct result of something I said, or did, or didn't do, or forgot to do or should have done. Some things are not my fault and some things are not my fight. I didn't know how to change the people around me because I didn't have the power to change anyone but me; I can only change myself. I am responsible for my own actions and choices, not the actions and choices of others.

WHAT LITTLE ME DIDN'T KNOW
IT WASN'T MY FAULT

WHAT BIG ME KNOWS NOW
I CAN ONLY CHANGE MYSELF

HOW I GOT THERE
I STOPPED BLAMING & STARTED FORGIVING

Parents are made to love us, and they do, but sometimes they don't know how to show it. Sometimes they don't love themselves. Sometimes we have to teach love to learn love. Sometimes we have to teach the ones meant to teach us. If your brothers and sisters are blaming you for their problems, it's not your fault. If your community is hurting you, it's not your fault. Those church members that were supposed to help you, well, maybe they aren't. It's not your fault so don't take it on as if it is. They may be suffering from their own illnesses or self-hatred. They may not have been taught the same things you are trying to learn now. They may have a story that you don't understand. Regardless, YOU can still be okay. YOU can be the change your community, your family and your friends need. Take responsibility for your own actions and let others own theirs.

MISTAKES ARE MADE, NOT ASSIGNED.

I can only control what I do, what I say, how I act, how I behave, how I treat others and how I let others treat me. The more responsibility I take for my life the brighter it will shine. The brighter I choose to shine determines the brightness of those around me, too.

My job is to make sure my life is the best I can make it. Just because I grew up poor doesn't mean I should resort to drugs to get through it. I had parents that weren't ready to be parents but that didn't mean I was unloved. Some of my friends chose a life of crime but I didn't have to make the same mistakes.

FOLLOW YOUR PASSION AND YOU WILL FIND YOUR TIME WELL SPENT.

I chose to do well in school and followed my dreams. That doesn't make me better than anyone I know; it means I try to make the best possible choices. My life is determined by the choices I make and the consequences I face because of them. If I make bad choices, the results are bad consequences. If I make good choices, the results are good consequences. The more bad choices I make, the harder it is to fight my way back. The more good choices I make, the easier my path will be. It's important for LITTLE YOU to understand that the choices you make now or in the near future can shape your life either positively or negatively.

It may not seem like choices made in childhood can affect your future. Most of them may not, but some of them do. The ones that can change your path in detrimental ways and have the potential to forever change your desired course are as follows: choosing to try drugs, engaging in unprotected sex, failing to do well in school, dropping out of school, stealing and/or joining a gang.

A Life Force exists inside of me; it shapes my life positively if I learn to tap into it and learn to use its strength. My choices are also based on my perception of the world. If I let others control me, they will. But if I take a stand for what is right, I am at peace. If I go for what I want, my desires are fulfilled. If I make the same decisions others made, I receive similar results. My Life Force is more powerful than any obstacle or circumstance I face because it is God-given and God makes no mistakes; therefore, I am not a mistake. Challenges will always end up in my path but it's okay because every time I overcome one, the next one becomes easier to navigate. One of the greatest gifts I learned was the ability to forgive; it was how I found my power. Forgiveness taught me that everything I do or say has the potential to not only impact me but everyone around me. My future success depended on my ability to forgive.

I learned to forgive my parents, I learned how to forgive my family, I learned to forgive myself. I forgave myself for my own mistakes so that I could forgive others for theirs. Forgiveness isn't about accepting what someone else did, it's about choosing to move forward rather than stay stuck. I practice forgiveness daily because each new day brings new pain that I need to resolve. We all make mistakes and we all need forgiveness. The pain I carry is pain I've also caused. Therefore, it works simultaneously to forgive yourself and forgive others. It opens the door to positive change and peace of mind.

SUFFERING SHOULD BE OVERCOME NOT REPEATED.

I had to learn the situations I was born into were not for me to blame and hate myself. I had teenage parents, a father in prison, a family affected by gang violence. None of this meant that I was unwanted or unloved. My responsibility is to own the choices I make and to not play victim to the ones I don't. Taking accountability and letting go of circumstances I can't change are stepping-stones to my happiness.

List (3) things you blame yourself for that might not be your fault.

1. _____

2. _____

3. _____

List activities you think girls your age should be doing. Start with your current age and add one year up until you are 18.

Girls _____ *years old should be* _____

Girls _____ *years old should be* _____

Girls _____ *years old should be* _____

Girls _____ *years old should be* _____

Girls _____ *years old should be* _____

Girls _____ *years old should be* _____

Girls _____ *years old should be* _____

Girls _____ *years old should be* _____

Girls _____ *years old should be* _____

Girls _____ *years old should be* _____

Girls _____ *years old should be* _____

List three things you do that make you happy.

1. _____

2. _____

3. _____

The same people who hurt you are the same people who teach you. You can learn from the mistakes others make or choose to make the same ones. If you want a different result, make a different choice. No matter what you do, learn as much as you can. Knowledge is power and power is freedom. Give yourself the gift of education.

CHAPTER THREE
IT'S MY CHOICE / KNOWLEDGE IS POWER

Knowledge is power and power is freedom. LITTLE YOU may feel like you have no control over your life right now, but you have more than you realize. Yes, I get it. In the ways you might imagine, you don't - LITTLE YOU can't decide where you live or buy anything you want or go wherever you please because you are under the care of others. But you can decide to go to school. You can fill your brain with information. You can learn from the world around you.

Your future starts now. Right now. Be dedicated to your studies and find out what you love to do. You're in school anyways, right? Then become the best student you can be. Focus on your schoolwork, your homework and learn everything you can - and don't judge yourself solely on your grades. If you pay attention, study and try hard - and you still get a C - love that C because you gave it your all and it doesn't mean you didn't learn. When you make mistakes, find out what you forgot or missed and try it again. If you don't know, ask. I promise you that if you educate yourself, you will wake up one day and realize you have attained the skills and tools necessary to be successful.

What do you want to be when you grow up?

Create your own opportunities by increasing your knowledge or else you will limit your potential – your level of education will decide for you. It will lead you to the life you want to create for yourself. I don't know where I would be if it wasn't for my studies or for my passion to dance. When I was your age, I had no idea how far either would take me, but every time I am on stage, teaching or creating. I am grateful to be living my dream. I am proud of myself for not giving up even when my lack of self-esteem would have warranted it. That is why I am begging you to not give up on yourself and to get an education. I want you to give yourself not only a fighting chance but also the strength to carry on because you deserve it.

MASTER YOUR MIND WITH KNOWLEDGE AND YOU WILL MASTER YOUR LIFE IN ACTION.

Knowledge is found in the classroom, in your home, at your friend's house, in the streets - it's all around you. And the best way to know yourself is to look to your past, design your own future and start heading in the direction you want to go. Under chaos, underprivileged, or under the care of others, you can still create your own future – by educating and empowering yourself.

This is the only time I will preach, beg, yell, plead or come off like the adults that annoy you, but it's for one reason and one reason only – it is the make or break of your life in so many ways. Education matters – knowledge is power and power is freedom. Don't let the freedom our ancestors fought for go to waste. They didn't have choices but you do. Choose education.

I'm not suggesting you have to be the best student in the class, or that you must pass every test with flying colors or that you can never receive a failing grade - it's about learning as much as you can, receiving the degrees that open doors and attaining the skills and tools necessary to do whatever it is you love to do. The more you know the better off you will be.

WHAT LITTLE ME DIDN'T KNOW
I HAVE CHOICES

WHAT BIG ME KNOWS NOW
POWER IS FREEDOM

HOW I GOT THERE
I GAINED KNOWLEDGE

BIG ME is telling you as a friend, not an authority. I care about you and want you to find your power and the best way to achieve it is through knowledge. You have the power to design your own destiny and the sooner you start, the faster you will not only get there, but also realize you have it. You are forced to go to school but only you have the power to do well. It's your choice whether or not to learn so please - learn, learn, and learn some more.

School is more than just receiving good or bad grades. It teaches you how to interact in a group, how to engage in critical thinking and how to socialize with your peers. Teachers are not always at the head of the class either and can be sitting at the desk next to you. Knowledge is everywhere if you look for it. Learn from mistakes as well. If you don't, you will keep facing the same problems until you find the lessons in them.

Discover your dreams and believe in them. Believe in yourself. Opportunities are right in front of you, but only if you are willing to go for it.

EDUCATION GIVES YOU CONTROL OVER YOUR LIFE; IGNORANCE GIVES OTHERS THE ABILITY TO CONTROL YOU.

Choose to be in control of yourself! Don't fall prey to oppression, suppression or depression. Be the change you want to see. In fact, I want you to do your own research. If you think I'm wrong then look around. Who do you admire? Are they educated? How did they create the life of success they have? Find out. Ask. Listen. Seek the answers that can help make your future exactly what you imagine it could be.

List 2 people that you admire and share why. Ask about their education, the steps they took and any other details that might help you understand how they got to where they are today.

1. _____

2. _____

There will always be people who want you to fail. It's sad but true. Don't let them. Education is your best defense and sometimes your only chance. Why do you think people weren't permitted to go to school and were denied the right to read? Because it is the quickest and easiest way to hold people down and strip them of the tools necessary to succeed. That's why education is so important – because oppression is based on fear and ignorance.

Don't strip yourself of your own power. Don't lose because you didn't try. You may not be in the richest or best schools, but chose to beat the odds. In fact, you are learning more than most because you are facing difficulties and challenges and surviving them. You are stronger for it. You have the will to survive. Fight for your place, your right and your future. No matter what, no matter how and no matter where - educate yourself. It's your choice and no one can take it away from you - except you. Make your future a bright one and not one full of hardship, struggle and stress. Education is Key.

ARM YOURSELF WITH KNOWLEDGE AND BE TWICE AS POWERFUL AS THE REST.

Ask some women about choices they regret that negatively affected their future. Write about them below.

Choices	Results

You can make all the same mistakes as those around you, but expect the same life as well. Or, you can try something different and give yourself a chance. It's your choice. Learn everything you can and learn from all available resources – your family, your community, your church and, of course, school. No matter what's going on for you right now, make your education work for you! It's the best defense against circumstances that leave you powerless. Knowledge is power!

My current GPA is ———— *. By the end of next semester I will raise it by* ———— *points. My goal by the end of the year is to have a GPA of* ————————————————

Do you need help with school? It's okay. Everyone does, even the smartest kids. Talk to your teachers and school counselors. Don't fall behind if you can help it. If you are behind, try to catch up. **You can choose to learn anytime and at a pace comfortable for you.** Here is a list of resources that may be helpful.

- Ask about free tutoring services **at school or through local programs.**
- Find neighbors who are willing to help.
- Go to the local library and find out what they have to offer.
- Go online and find information on the subject you find difficult.

Don't be afraid to ask for help. Everyone needs help and your future is on the line.

Some of what kept me from liking school was the voices in my head that put me down, tore me down and wore me down. Do you know what I'm talking about? I'm talking about my chatterbox. My chatterbox was the biggest bully I'd ever met.

CHAPTER FOUR
MY CHATTERBOX / MY FLATTER BOX

So what is my chatterbox? It's the nickname I gave those annoying and negative thoughts that invade my head, you know, the voices that put me down, call me names and tell me lies. It's my internal bully who tells me I'm fat, ugly, stupid, unloved, unwanted, pathetic and unliked or (fill in any negative descriptor). It's sly, cruel, loud and horrific. My chatterbox is so brutal it has told me that I don't even have the right to live.

Do you have a bully in your head? What does it say? Pay attention and write down what it tells you and how often you hear it.

Why do I have an internal dialogue that seems to be against me? Honestly, I don't know. I'm not sure where it came from, when it started or why I have it, but it's there nonetheless. Its goal is to keep me from my greatness. Filled with past resentments, future fears and painful memories, it tears me down, wears me down and keeps me down. It is the source of my low self-esteem and is damaging me in every way.

Our negative thoughts originate from different places but usually begin when we're very young. We internalize and attach negative descriptors because of something we heard, thought we heard, believed was true or was told to be true. The more critical the people around us, the louder the voices become. The more verbal abuse we endure, the more damage is done to our psyche. We need to change the insults into positive beliefs so that we believe the right things. We have to overcome our minds.

My chatterbox contains it all: lies, painful remarks, false beliefs, misinterpretations and miscommunications. It's unnerving how quickly the thoughts come and how little I ignore them. It never occurred to me to question them in the past; they were so convincing I just assumed them to be true.

THE ABILITY TO CHANGE YOUR THOUGHTS GIVES YOU THE ABILITY TO CHANGE YOUR REALITY.

So how do I handle my chatterbox? Well, luckily for me, I met a woman who saw it, understood it and told me all about it. She said, "You are wonderfully made. You are Divine. You have the potential of the entire Universe inside of you." She then explained how my thoughts and my feelings were mine and just because someone says something mean to me, or criticizes me or points fingers at me doesn't force me to hold on to whatever it was that was said or done. Or, more importantly, doesn't require me to repeat them to myself over and over again. At some point, I detached the feeling from the original remark and made it my own when I could have changed it or discarded it instead.

After that day, I started paying attention and took note of my thoughts throughout the day. It was quite shocking to discover - it really was me! I was the one calling myself names, listening to the lies and believing them to be true. I was the one looking around and seeking out ways to confirm their reality. It was devastating to realize that it really was me who was hurting - me.

WHAT LITTLE ME DIDN'T KNOW
I TELL MYSELF LIES

WHAT BIG ME KNOWS NOW
I CAN CHANGE MY THOUGHTS

HOW I GOT THERE
DAILY POSITIVE AFFIRMATIONS

After the shock wore off that I was my own bully, I became grateful because I had found the source of my chatterbox's power - me! My chatterbox had power only because I gave it power. And if I gave it power then I could take away its power. So that's what I did. I changed my negative thoughts into positive affirmations. I repeated my affirmations daily and it didn't matter if I believed them or not because at first I didn't. In fact, I felt ridiculous saying them out loud. All that mattered was that I said them. I had to give myself compliments and show myself kindness. And guess what? It worked.

To this day, I've never quite exterminated my chatterbox but it has gotten quieter and quieter and sometimes it actually has become silent. When the voices do come, I change them. I challenge you to try it. Change your chatterbox into your flatter box like I did. Instead of telling myself I am fat, ugly and stupid, I change my thoughts to curvy, beautiful and intelligent. If I hear the words unloved I say loved, unwanted I say desired, unworthy I say deserving. Basically, I change every negative thought into a positive one and I do it until I believe it.

Changing my chatterbox changed my reality because my thoughts design my reality. Positive affirmations build self-esteem while negative comments generate self-hate. I hope LITTLE YOU understands what BIG ME is saying because, trust and believe, it matters. So be kind to yourself and start building a beautifully strong image of yourself - one that tells you to hold your head high and fills you with self-respect and self-love. If you do, LITTLE YOU will become unstoppable and you will accomplish even the most far fetched dreams. It's true, I promise! Start now. Tell yourself how beautiful, amazing and powerful you are and one day you will finally believe it!

It no longer matters what others believe about me; the only thing that matters is what I tell myself.

To understand the damage my chatterbox inflicted, I needed to see it in action and not just hear it so I taped a photograph of myself when I was five years old to my wall next to my bed.

Whenever I heard the voices putting me down, I walked over to the picture and looked at the little girl and I started telling her the same things I was telling myself. Do you know what happened? I couldn't do it. I couldn't look at that girl and tell her she was ugly, stupid or unloved. That would be mean! Instead I would start telling her how amazing and beautiful she was. By doing this exercise, it occurred to me that when I would say mean things to myself it was the same thing as telling that little girl – because that little girl is me. It may sound silly and ridiculous but it taught me to be kinder to myself because everyone should feel the affects that compliments bring. No child should face harsh critics like the one I had in my head.

I can't stop the world from being cruel, but I can prevent myself from participating in it. I have the power to change my thoughts and that changes my reality. If my world is gloomy then my thoughts need brightening. I can restart my day, my week or my life anytime, in any moment, for any given reason if I make a conscious effort to do so. All it takes is for me to stop and be grateful, remind myself to be thankful and remember to appreciate how beautiful life can be.

I'm grateful that woman entered my life that day and taught me to see myself differently. She gave me permission to believe better things for myself. Thanks to her I had a new way of thinking and a new vision for my life. I let a tiny bit of the Light in and the entire world lit up. My life transformed. Loving myself encouraged me to love others, too. I had to first accept myself before I could accept those around me. All love starts with self-love.

If someone in your life is constantly putting you down or calling you names and you ask them to stop, and you are unable to remove yourself from their presence, then the best thing you can do is not believe them. When they say something hurtful, immediately tell yourself the opposite, positive affirmation. People can be critical for different reasons but no reason makes it right. Please don't believe them. You are a beautiful, loved, strong girl who deserves encouragement and support. Find women out there who will show you kindness and spend as much time with them as you can.

Positive affirmations are stepping-stones toward defining who I am and who I want to become. Not only do I say them to myself, I affirm the women in my life, too. It's always nice to receive a compliment and I never receive more compliments than I need. In fact, I hear more criticism than anyone should and that holds true for most people.

YOU ARE THE MOST VALUABLE PIECE WITHIN YOUR OWN HUMAN REVOLUTION.

Imagine the moment that someone tells you that you are beautiful, amazing, gifted, talented, loved and needed! Well, I am. I hope this moment is your moment, too, like the moment I had years ago. LITTLE ME became BIG ME that day. The day I gave myself the permission to believe in my greatness was the day I found a new outlook on the world. It was the day I met me and all that I had to offer for the first time.

What does your chatterbox tell you?

I AM _____

I AM _____

I AM _____

Create your flatter box by writing the opposite, positive belief about yourself.

Chatterbox	Flatterbox

Read from the flatter box list you created every day for a month. Even if you don't believe the words, just give yourself permission to say them. Say them no matter what is going on inside of you. Eventually, it will change. It may feel awkward, or silly, or ridiculous at first but I promise it will change and I don't make promises I can't keep. I promise you that one day when you are saying those kind words to yourself you will find that you believe them. It's magical!

Find your favorite picture from when you were five years old. Tape it to your wall. If you start telling yourself mean things, look at the picture and tell that little girl the same things. You can't so start telling yourself all the loving things you wish somebody told you.

I am no longer at the mercy of my own chatterbox. I have the power to control what I think. I have the choice to change my outlook. I am my own boss and I am in charge of my own well being. That's right! I'm no longer forced to succumb to the voices that try to tear me down, keep me stuck or hold me hostage. I refuse to be taken down by my own self. And if I can change my thoughts then I can change my feelings, too, because feelings are not facts.

CHAPTER FIVE

FEELINGS AREN'T FACTS / RESPOND, DON'T REACT

Like the lies I store in my chatterbox, I have feelings that aren't based on facts. My thoughts and feelings are intertwined and so my thoughts affect my feelings and my feelings affect my thoughts. They play off one another and impact one another. Positive thoughts generate positive feelings and positive feelings create a positive life.

Let me better explain. If I listen to my chatterbox and it's telling me I am fat and ugly then my feelings will be a mixture of jealousy, sadness and anger. If I believe I am confident and beautiful, my feelings coincide and I become happy, content and grateful. What I think determines how I feel and how I feel influences the choices I make. That's why changing my chatterbox to my flatter box was crucial to my well-being. If I hadn't, and negative thoughts generate negative feelings and negative feelings lead to negative actions – then I was in a whole lot of trouble – and I was. My thoughts were undermining my attempts at ridding myself of the uncomfortable feelings that plagued me.

FEELINGS ARE MEANT TO BE GUIDES AND NOT REASONS TO ATTACK MYSELF.

I used to believe every feeling mattered. I also believed that whatever I was feeling at any given time was how I always felt. For instance, if I was sad I never felt anything but sad. Because of these misbeliefs, my feelings became bigger than they were intended to be and harder to control than they should have been. Feelings aren't facts; they are neither true nor false and aren't rational nor logical. I'm not suggesting I should ignore or discount how I feel but rather acknowledge my feelings and then make a decision about what to do. Feelings do come and go and my current feeling will always pass.

It took awhile for me to fully grasp that my feelings didn't require immediate attention or instant action. In fact, my feelings are designed to be guides only; they inform me whether or not I'm living my truth and alert me if I'm not. They aren't meant to be in charge of my every action. They let me know when I've tipped the scales too far either way. In other words, feelings help me gauge if I'm hanging out with the right people, doing the right things and going to the right places. They are personal clues suggesting I continue, warning me to slow down or demanding me to stop. By checking in with myself regularly, I monitor how my thoughts and actions are affecting me, how my feelings are affecting my choices and whether or not adjustments need to be made.

Any feeling I experience already exists inside of me. Therefore, I can't blame anyone for making me feel. For example, no one can make me mad but a person's actions or words may cause me to feel mad. How I handle my anger is then up to me. I have the choice to react to it or respond. Responding is the better choice because it leads to wiser decisions. It allows the feeling to subside and the rational side of me to emerge. I have the right to feel any way I want but I don't have the right to be rude.

Not every feeling makes sense and not every feeling needs to be analyzed. If I consistently feel the same feeling then it's telling me to take note. Additionally, if I'm having the same feelings regarding the same person, place or thing then I should stop and question why that is. Most likely, I'm receiving warning signals suggesting I remove that person, place or thing or I'm in need of an attitude adjustment before I get resentful.

Feelings come and go and I'd rather respond than react to them. When I react, I make impulsive decisions that typically don't turn out well. I end up apologizing and embarrassing myself. But when I respond, because I have given myself a chance to step back and look at the bigger picture, I make wiser choices. I also make it a rule never to make major life decisions when I'm angry or depressed. I also wait a specific number of minutes to call, text or email someone after they've upset me to be sure my feelings haven't changed. Communicating feelings properly is very important. I try not to hold everything in nor do I blurt every feeling out. I sit with my feelings first, then find the courage to share them and problem solve with any person who has upset me. My goal is to avoid confronting people in rage, but be honest, direct, and clear about what my boundaries are.

FEELINGS CAN BE NUMBED BUT THE NUMBNESS WILL WEAR OFF.

There are times, too, when I attach past situations to current feelings. For example, I may be feeling sad because my best friend forgot my birthday. That is a valid reason to feel sad. Everyone wants to be acknowledged on their birthday and especially by their best friend. However, instead of feeling sad, I tell myself my friend forgot because I am unloved and unwanted. Somewhere in my past an event triggered a connection and my chatterbox created the insult to be used against me. Now, every time I feel sad, I attach the same descriptors to myself (in this case, unloved and unwanted) whether it fits the current situation or not.

Attaching old feelings to current situations is unintentional and happens subconsciously. It may feel as natural as sweating when hot yet it isn't natural at all. I learned to tell myself a different story than the one that was actually being told. I created the cycle unknowingly and it continued unnecessarily.

When my friend forgot my birthday she never told me I was unloved or unwanted. I did. Why? I don't know. Maybe someone said those things in my past. Maybe I thought I heard someone say those things. Maybe someone told me someone said those things. Maybe I told myself them because it made the most sense at the time to explain what happened. Maybe my chatterbox made it up. Pinpointing the reason helps but it isn't necessary to understand the mistake. No matter why it happened, unloved and unwanted became stored in my body as the reasons I feel sad. The truth was that my friend forgot my birthday - that's it. Accepting this without the need to attack my self-worth is the healthy way to handle the situation. Problem was I didn't know it back then.

MY MEMORY IS NOT A PERFECT RECORDING.

Finding the healthy path to handling my feelings is tricky. There are many factors at play – there are my thoughts, my feelings, the intensity of my feelings, and its many complicated patterns designed to protect me from pain overload, how other people respond to my feelings, how I respond to their response and so on and so forth. It can be too much to handle at times and too difficult to navigate.

The important element is knowing that every feeling doesn't excuse drama and every action doesn't require intense emotion. I have found that the key is to ask, "what is the truth?" Let the truth of the circumstance lead in resolving the conflict.

I was controlled more by my thoughts than my feelings which is the reason why I had to change my chatterbox to my flatter box. Others, however, are ruled more by the feelings they encounter which then influences their thoughts and actions. Both are intertwined and both impact each other so a healthy mental outlook and a healthy maintenance of emotion are necessary to live a happy, healthy lifestyle.

Do your feelings or your thoughts influence you the most? Are you in control or do they control you?

If I pay attention to my thoughts and make an effort to think more positively than negatively, if I stick to my moral and ethical code, and if I seek compassion in those around me and treat others fairly, then my feelings will stay relatively in check. Like I said before, moments when my feelings erupt are bound to happen but they are far and few between. If I surround myself with liars and mean people, and if I am unhappy and perceive everything negatively all the time, then I will experience a very different world because my feelings will bear down on others and bring misery. We all need to throw our own pity party at times but it becomes too draining to be around people who do nothing but complain. Life throws curveballs to all of us and everyone feels more pain than we'd like but each of us also has the choice to let go, adapt, change, accept, forgive or move on. It's our human responsibility.

FORGIVENESS REQUIRES THE COURAGE TO OPEN YOUR HEART AND BE LED BY LOVE.

Connecting my thoughts and my feelings helps me lead a more confident and insightful life. It comes with time and practice so be gentle on yourself. Awareness and willingness open the gates to growth and the rest will fall into place as long as I keep at it.

WHAT LITTLE ME DIDN'T KNOW
FEELINGS AREN'T FACTS

WHAT BIG ME KNOWS NOW
FEELINGS ARE GUIDES

HOW I GOT THERE
I STOPPED REACTING & STARTED RESPONDING

Feelings are designed to keep me in check and I am responsible for monitoring them. I can choose to listen and take appropriate action to ensure a happier life or I can ignore them and find myself in situations I never intended to be.

If I choose to ignore my feelings at some point and in some way, they will resurface again, no matter what I do to escape the pain. Until I process my feelings and actively choose make a change.

BIG ME recognizes that feelings come and feelings go. It's important to acknowledge them but it's not okay to be controlled by them. They aren't meant to be reasons I dislike myself. If I am hurt, I'm hurt and I challenge myself to heal. If I am angry, I'm angry; I'm better off not reacting. It's best to respond if I can. My feelings let me know whether or not I am saying, behaving or doing things that are leading me to happiness, peace of mind and usefulness.

So how do I trust my feelings or my thoughts? First, I had to stop and listen to my inner dialogue and tune in to my internal self. I had to learn to identify the difference between feelings versus thoughts. By asking myself questions I started to get to know myself better - do my thoughts make sense for the way I feel? Do my feelings feel bigger than the situation at hand? Do I feel sad or tired or angry most of the time? Am I saying something only a bully would say? Am I in control or do I feel out of control?

If I regret something I said, or feel guilty for something I've done, or am disappointed for something I failed to accomplish, then my feelings are telling me that I'm choosing behaviors that aren't leading me in the right direction. They are telling me to make changes if I want to feel differently.

Growth always requires change.

Do I want to let go and move on or hold on and suffer? I can try to make changes and experience a different way of living or I can stay stuck and expect the same results in return. I can blame myself or blame others or find solutions and work toward solving problems. I can change my thoughts to change my feelings or change my actions to change my thoughts. My internal self requires attention and the more I check in the better my life becomes.

Write down the feelings that you feel most often. Are they positive or negative? What thoughts coincide with them?

_____

_____

_____

If you could feel any way, what is the feeling you would most want to experience and why?

_____

_____

_____

Feelings aren't facts, only guides. Understanding your feelings is key to working through them. If your feelings create negative self-talk then you, too, are stuck believing lies. Find people who celebrate you and bring out your best side. The people in your life play a big part in how you see yourself and influence the choices you make. Remember to choose wisely because you are the company you keep.

CHAPTER SIX
YOU ARE WHO YOU KEEP / HAVING GREAT FRIENDS

Friends are the people I choose to have in my life; they are the family I create. I can change my friends at any time for any reason; they are my choice and I can make any choice I wish. The same holds true in return because unlike family, my friends have the right to cut me off. Therefore, it is equally important to be a good friend as it is to have good friends.

FRIENDS EARN THEIR PLACE IN YOUR LIFE; YOU EARN YOUR PLACE IN THEIR LIVES, TOO.

I have friends from different places, for different lengths of time and for many different reasons. Each person is important and each plays a role; they teach, guide, help, support, encourage, comfort and entertain. They are the people I have the most fun with and with whom I share my deepest sorrows. They have the most influence over my life and can determine the course I take. It is important to surround myself with the right people.

Choose friends wisely. Hanging out with the wrong people can affect your life permanently. Those around you influence you. In fact, your brain is designed to conform, so surround yourself with solid people who have your best interest at heart. Look for quality not quantity; the five most important people in your life will determine the course you take.

I have friends from different places, for different lengths of time and for many different reasons. Each person is important and each plays a role; they teach, guide, help, support, encourage, comfort and entertain. They are the people I have the most fun with and with whom I share my deepest sorrows. They have the most influence over my life and can determine the course I take. It is important to surround myself with the right people.

Choosing friends is an important process; if I don't choose wisely it could cause me trouble. I might hang out with people who are leading me away from my goals, convincing me to do things that go against who I am or who keep me locked in a life I don't really want. People influence us more than we imagine and even when I say I will never be like some girl, if I hang out with her for too long I will eventually become more like her. We unknowingly pick up the habits of our friends. If someone makes poor decisions then I start making poor decisions, too. I have to be careful whom I spend my time with because eventually you are whom you keep. I want to be around girls who bring me joy not pain, growth not digression and kindness not cruelty because I want to be happy, I want to be kind and I want to be successful. My friends determine whether or not I will be the person I am intended to be.

You don't need permission from anyone to move forward.

I have a handful of best friends, a pocketful of good friends and a number of friends and/or acquaintances. My greatest and most important friends are my best friends who I like to call, "My Girls!" My girls show me more respect, support, love, care, courage, fun, sympathy and understanding than anyone else. I value them as much as I value myself. Therefore, as I learn to value myself more and more – I find the people around me becoming more valued and quality people, too. We attract what we are or who can teach us what we need to learn.

You attract friends who are similar to you. The better friend you are, the better friends you will have. It's important to value yourself and be a quality person so you can attract quality people into your life. Find friends you trust with your life, friends who teach you about life and friends who will walk beside you no matter what's going on in your life. Your friends matter because you matter.

My best friends influence my life to such a degree it's crucial to have the right ones. I can survive anything with a strong support system. My girls are the girls that lead me forward and never leave me behind. They are the ones who want the best for me and will be there for me when I'm not at my best. It's important whom I consider best friends because I depend on them when all else fails. All friends are important but my best friends are the most important people in my life.

When choosing my best friends, it takes time because only experience can determine if they have the qualities a best friend requires. I need time to hang out and watch whom they are, how they act and where they want to go. I need to get to know them, observe them in action, notice how they treat each other, discover how they treat me alone and around others, place trust in them and determine if they are trustworthy, disagree and find out if they can survive it, and be myself around them and wait to see if I am truly accepted or not. It takes life experiences to find out if they will stand by me.

When I choose friends who aren't sincere – and this does happen - I must be willing to let them go. I must have the courage to stand-alone until I find my true allies. It's not easy, trust me, I've been through it. In fact, as a LITTLE ME, I had to learn this lesson and it was one of the most painful and difficult times in my life. It was brutal.

When I was young, I grew up dancing with a bunch of girls and we all had fun together. As we got older, however, our interests changed and so did our friendship. I wanted to do well in school and become a great dancer but they wanted to drop out and roam the streets instead. One day we were tight and the next day they were gone. They laughed at me and called me names for the choices I made and I couldn't become who they wanted me to be either so we separated. It was the first time I felt betrayed by girls I trusted. I was left alone through it all because they all stuck together. It was awful finding out that I was not only different from the girls I thought had the perfect lives, but I was different from the girls I thought were just like me, too. It was confusing and hard to handle.

Looking back, they taught me a valuable lesson. They taught me that friends come and go but my passion and my life are mine to own. I was devastated but, luckily for me, I stayed my course and today I am living my dream because of it. I chose not to follow the crowd and remain true to myself. I had to do it alone but it was the best choice I ever made. I'm not sure what happened to those girls but the girls who befriended me shortly thereafter are still in my life today. They, like me, had dreams and we continue to support each other as we meet, discover and create new goals to accomplish. If I had gone against my true nature and followed my group of friends back then, I might have ended up in a life I never wanted but because I stuck to what I believed in, I have a life I designed just for me. I hope those girls found their dreams, too, and if not, I hope they have the chance to change their paths and find it soon. Sometimes the hardest moments can turn into the most beautiful blessings.

WHAT LITTLE ME DIDN'T KNOW
FRIENDS INFLUENCE ME

WHAT BIG ME KNOWS NOW
I CHOOSE MY FRIENDS

HOW I GOT THERE
I CHOSE ME AND THEN MADE GREAT FRIENDS

You are who you keep so look around at those who surround you. Do they have what you want? Do they treat you kindly? Do they give and take, teach and learn, forgive and forget, tend and defend, and love and support? If so, you are destined for greatness and they will help you get there. If not, then you are still destined for greatness but have a greater chance of ending up in a life that you never wanted, you couldn't imagine or you don't understand. Change your friends when necessary to change your life for the better. Don't keep friends who do you wrong; all you need is a handful of true friends to get through.

The five people closest to me are the five people who I depend on the most. If the five are all at the best friend status, I am incredibly blessed. If those five are a combination of best friends and good friends, I am lucky. If any of those five aren't true friends, I am setting myself up for failure. Today, BIG ME chooses to surround myself with positive people because negative people bring negative outcomes. My friends deserve me to be the best and I deserve to have friends that are the best. And, thankfully, I do.

The five people you keep closest to you are the five who will determine who you are, who you become and where you will go. Choose your five wisely. Choose your five for the right reasons. List your five (parents shouldn't be included on this list because they play their own unique roles in our lives).

1. _____

2. _____

3. _____

4. _____

5. _____

Write next to their name their 3 best qualities and the 3 ways they add the most value to your life.

1. _____

2. _____

3. _____

Write down 3 additional friends who add value or share an interest with you. Write next to their names their best quality and the way they add value or what interest they share.

1. _____

2. _____

3. _____

Are any of your 5 or 3 not a positive influence in your life?
If so, who and for what reason?

_____

_____

_____

List 3 people who might have you in their circle of 5. What are your 3 best qualities and how do you add value to their life?

1. _____

2. _____

3. _____

List some ways you could become a better friend.

_____

_____

_____

It's amazing how much the rest of my life takes care of itself when I surround myself with women I trust. There have been times, however, when I felt alone and when I've stood alone – but I didn't like it. I had to learn how to be alone. Choosing to be alone meant learning to like my own company.

CHAPTER SEVEN
BEING ALONE / MEDITATION

Feeling alone describes feeling different and alienated from the rest of the world. Being alone isn't a feeling; it's an action. It's a conscious decision to spend time with myself so I can discover who I am, what I want and where I'm going; it's how I get to know my authentic self. If I don't want to spend time with myself why would anyone else want to spend time with me?

When I choose to be alone, I like to meditate. Meditation is a practice used to quiet the mind and relax the body. It helps me to feel connected to the truth. Practicing meditation is a personal and private experience but it can be experienced in a group setting as well. The best way to explain it is to describe what it means to me.

Typically, I find a quiet room and I sit by myself with my legs crossed and my back upright. Nobody is around to prevent any influence or pressure brought on by other people's opinions or thoughts. The room is also void of outside distractions by turning off televisions, video games or any other object that might beg for my attention. It's about wanting to be only with myself so I can explore who I am, what I want, where I'm at and where I'm going.

Once the room is clear, I sit quietly and breathe. I inhale long, deep breaths inviting the positive energy of the universe in and I exhale long, deep breaths releasing any negative energy stored within my body. I focus on my breathe and I breathe in and I breathe out until I feel the outside world fade away and my inner self awaken. I do this until I sense the relaxation throughout and I feel everything a sense of stillness. I am reaching my center at this point. I feel my spirit and I honor it by staying still. Then, I listen to the messages I receive without censoring them. I hear what I need to hear no matter what it is. Sometimes it's chaotic and I am unable to quiet my thoughts but I allow it to be and get the message I need to hear. That is, I learn that changes are needed to bring me back to a place of calm. Sometimes I hear messages of what I wish for or need to do. Sometimes I hear nothing and that is the most peaceful moments I ever have experienced. Whatever the message, I take note and I listen. I also use this time to say positive affirmations to myself or to talk to my higher power. I ask questions and make requests. I can do anything I want with my time during meditation as long as my intention is to find and maintain the healthiest sense of self that I can.

Meditation is different each time and can be different from person to person. It's okay. The point is to learn about yourself and you will if you are patient with the process. Trust me, I had no idea what I was doing when I first started and it was really uncomfortable. I felt silly and scared and couldn't sit still for long. Over time, it became less uncomfortable and I thoroughly enjoy it now but I, too, still have a lot to learn about it.

It's in these quiet moments that I learn about me by me. Too much time is spent being influenced and persuaded by outside sources (Media and Social Media etc) that the time I spend with myself is vital to living within my truest nature. However, I can't live in my true self if I don't know what it is which is why I spend quiet time alone. It's the only way I find discover the real me.

I never enjoyed feeling alone but I've learned to love being alone. In fact, if I don't spend time with myself I become grumpy and irritable. It's become such a necessary piece to my overall well being that I know when it's been too long since I've last enjoyed it. Don't get me wrong - it was awkward and uncomfortable at first but now I have a better sense and I understand not only why I do it but why I need to do it to be happy.

WHAT LITTLE ME DIDN'T KNOW
IT'S OKAY TO BE ALONE

WHAT BIG ME KNOWS NOW
I LIKE MY OWN COMPANY

HOW I GOT THERE
I SPENT TIME MEDITATING

Don't be discouraged if it takes some time for you to understand how to meditate. It's a process and when it happens you will know it. Show patience and gentleness to yourself because, ultimately, that is what it is teaching you to do in all aspects of your life.

How can we challenge our need to panic or be in rage? Next time you are scared or anxious, try breathing. Breathe in deeply and breathe out slowly. You will feel your body relax, your thoughts slow and your panic subside. Focusing on your breath is like listening for a divine voice.. It's amazing!

Being alone includes other activities as well. Sometimes, I do dream work. I make collages and vision boards of things I want, places I want to go and things I want to do. Or, I may sit and visualize my dreams in my head or write about them on paper. I carefully consider what I'm thinking about, how I'm feeling and whether or not my actions and behaviors are in or out of sync with my heart's desire. I imagine my dreams coming true because what I can see I can make happen.

Being alone also is a time to practice my faith as well. I am grateful for my spiritual upbringing because it has given me the comfort needed to get through challenging times. My faith aligns me with a Higher Power and a Higher Purpose; it's the belief in knowing that no matter what circumstances or conditions I face, I will be okay. I get lost on my path but I always find my way back; all I can do is walk in crooked lines until I get there. That's the key to faith – believing in something greater than myself in order to fulfill your destiny. If I have that, then I have the foundation from which to build.

Everyone has the freedom to choose the spiritual path that works best for them. No matter what path you or your family chooses is okay. Be centered in love, peace, and compassion for yourself and others and be determined to be the best possible human being and your life will be full of peace and many joyful days. It is the key to hope and continued growth. Without my faith I am fearful, but with it I am powerful.

Faith is a personal choice; some people are outspoken about their beliefs while others practice privately. Faith is built around different religious practices; there is no wrong way only your way. Find a faith that works for you. My faith has been my saving grace; it centers me and is the source of my comfort, my self-esteem, my acts of service towards others, my guidance and my inner truth.

Being alone is about me time – praying, meditating, writing, enjoying an activity, journaling, reading – anything that helps me connect my head with my heart, my external actions with my internal dialogue, and my faith with my center – in order to keep myself on track and on course. The more time I spend with myself, the more time I spend addressing my inner challenges. This helps build strength to always move forward. When I deny myself the opportunity for me time, I become lost, confused and out of touch with my goals, needs and desires.

Being alone teaches me to tap into my Life Force and to discover my role in making this world a better place. It happens one thought at a time and one action at a time. BIG ME has learned to enjoy my own company and love who I am. That is what I was designed to do: to be Divine and to be a powerful presence in the Universe.

Loving yourself is the process to becoming complete.

Quieting my thoughts and slowing my body takes practice and effort. It doesn't matter where or how you find peace and relaxation as long as you create a space that you feel calm in. We all need a calm place to center ourselves because life throws us curve balls and knocks us off balance. We need a place to get back on track and straighten out. Peace and tranquility are the stepping-stones to contentment.

Breathing in and breathing out can change any moment and put you back into a frame of mind where you can think clearer. Being with oneself is the only way to know oneself. Otherwise you are defined and controlled by those around you. Find your true nature and share it with the world.

Sitting alone can be frightening to some people, we are all so used to being consumed in the noise of the world. Sometimes that noise helps rationalize the lies, push feelings down and keep us as distracted as possible. I am happier if I focus my energy on the right course of action. Being alone is about learning to live my truth in my everyday life to the best of my ability. Fear has power if I give it power. Faith is powerful even when I forget to believe in it.

Is spending time with yourself uncomfortable and scary? If so, what about it leads you to feel that way?

_____

_____

_____

Where is your quiet and safe place for meditation? If you don't have one yet imagine it. You can create any environment just by using your mind. Give it a try and tell me about it.

_____

_____

_____

MEDITATION

Find a quiet place to sit or lay still and relax your whole body. Focus on your breath by feeling each breath connecting to the next one. Relax your thoughts. Sit and listen to your internal dialogue. Practice this 5 minutes or more per day. Share with your family and friends. Keep a journal of your experience to see how you grow throughout the process.

Meditation looks different to everyone but the ultimate goal is the same – learn to love myself as I was destined to be loved. Once that process is under way, spending time alone becomes more comfortable and in fact, becomes desired. BIG ME spends quality time with myself in other ways as well. I do activities I like, I am of service to others, and I enjoy nature and the gifts the world has to offer. Loving myself leads me to believe that nothing is impossible because I'M POSSIBLE!

CHAPTER EIGHT
IT'S IMPOSSIBLE / I'M POSSIBLE

Everything used to feel impossible. Everything was hard. Everything felt not so good. Once I realized that my life was my choice, my thoughts and feelings were up to me, and how I behaved was in my control, everything became possible. In fact, I became possible, that's what the word spells - I'M POSSIBLE! And if I'm possible, then nothing is impossible!

After reading this book, if you feel no different, it's okay. If you feel like the world opened up for you, it has. Most of you are most likely feeling something down the middle and that is exactly where you're meant to be. Lessons come when we're ready and everything happens for a reason. As long as we desire progress in our life, it will find us. Once it does, it's up to us to do the work to make it happen. That's what changes IMPOSSIBLE into I'M POSSIBLE!

I hope your negative thoughts and feelings will subside and you learn to use some of the tools to create the life you dream about each day. Your life is your choice. You choose how to think, how to feel, who you hang out with, how you behave, whether or not you are in control or hand it over to someone else, what you believe in, if you practice your faith and anything at all that has to do with you. Situations and circumstances are not always in your control, but your integrity and your character are.

THERE IS NOTHING - ABSOLUTELY NOTHING - THAT YOU CANNOT DO. IF YOU CAN BELIEVE IT THEN YOU CAN ACHIEVE IT.

Sometimes bad things happen to good people, it is just the way life is pain is inevitable. You will get hurt. Whether you choose to react or respond, cower or find power, fight or run, stand up or bend over, is up to you. How you come out of the fire is what matters the most. In the middle of the chaos life can give make a determination that you will come out stronger. Nothing is impossible when you believe in yourself and start telling yourself I'M POSSIBLE. When you actually believe it, your life will have no choice but to take off. Go ahead - live in your greatness – it's yours to have and yours to keep. Celebrate life. Celebrate those around you and their gifts. Miserable people want misery for others but joyful people want joy for everyone they encounter. Energy is contagious, be a joyful one! Stand out from the crowd by what you do. Let your life be an example. Say what you mean and mean what you say. Be Courageous. Be accountable and be responsible. It makes a difference. It really does!

Remember to be gentle to yourself and remain open. Be honest and be kind. We learn lessons when we are ready so you don't have to force what you're not ready to face. Your life starts now no matter how young or old you are and your life is your responsibility no matter how far off the path you go.

Control what you can - your education, your actions and your words. Say nice things to yourself and don't believe the lies others try to sell you. Dream big and take steps toward those dreams. Surround yourself with people who get you, who love you, who have fun with you and who call you out when you are making bad decisions. You deserve it! You are possible. I'M POSSIBLE!

I am already proud of you, the amazing things you will accomplish and the future generations you will inspire. Record your journey. LITTLE YOU is becoming the most wonderful, most powerful BIG YOU that you can be. Tell yourself affirmations until you believe it! Your life will prove itself to be great, I am not saying it will be easy, nothing in life is easy, but every challenge will make you grow stronger. Just don't ever give up!

Don't wait for opportunities to be given - go out and make them happen. You don't need permission from anyone to change and impact the world. Pray for the vision, the resources and the people needed to help accomplish your dreams.

Now, let's recap what I shared throughout this book about my continuous road to happiness and success. The first thing to remember is all love begins with self-love. If we accept ourselves, we don't seek validation from others. Not everyone needs to be in our circle of friends, but everyone has the right to be who they are regardless. If we want to surround ourselves with quality people, then we must first become a quality person. Every choice has a consequence and every action has an effect. The closer we are to our true nature, the better our choices and results will be. It's truly up to us to make our lives the happiest, most fulfilling, most useful they can be. It's not up to anyone else and we are not responsible for others. We are responsible, however, for becoming a good example for future generations, for living a life we deserve, for spreading love not hate, for fulfilling our dreams and for supporting those who surround us. If we do that, our lives will be happy, useful and full of hope for the future and all it has to offer. Be kind to yourself and the kindness in the world will find you. And never be afraid to fight for your right to live freely.

I felt alone until I realized I wasn't – I had to listen to others, share my story and be willing to tell the truth to get there. Once I heard the words "me too," I knew that others got me. We may look different on the outside and experience different lifestyles, but ultimately, we are more similar than not. If you have feelings, your feelings are no different than anyone else's. Pain and Joy are universal. Everything is not my fault nor should I pretend it to be. I mistakenly took on other people's choices and feelings as something I did or didn't do. I disliked myself because of things I couldn't control. I had to learn to become accountable for my behaviors and choices only. I also had to learn to let go of things I could not control – like other people. The better choices I made, the better outcome for my life.

Knowledge is power and power is freedom. Education, unity and action are the best weapon. It doesn't guarantee a rich lifestyle or unending wealth, but it gives you options to make an impact in your community and to create what you want to see.

Don't self-criticize, I had to change my chatterbox into my flatter box. I was the one tearing myself down and so I was responsible for building myself up instead. I gave myself positive affirmations no matter how awkward it felt until I believed them. I did and that changed my outlook on the rest of the world. My flatter box is the greatest gift I ever gave myself.

My feelings were controlling my actions and I had to reclaim my control over them. They are my guides and not my dictators. I check in with myself regularly to make sure I am heading in the direction I want to go. Feelings aren't facts and yet feelings provide a lot of information for me to live by. They are an important piece to my overall wellbeing. The five closest people in my life decide the course my life will take. Therefore, I have to choose wisely and, thankfully, I have. I still make the wrong friends but I let go of them much quicker. I value and cherish the friends who are my true allies. I am lucky for the wonderful people in my life and I am blessed for the paths I have crossed. I have so many wonderful teachers and each and every one of them is a gift. I work at being a good friend so I can keep the wonderful friends I have.

Spending time with myself has become an essential piece to my well being. I enjoy spending time with me. I meditate to discover my truest self. I find the courage to listen to the messages of whether or not I am doing the right things, hanging out with the right people or going in the right direction. I need alone time and I seek it out. That, in and of itself, is huge growth for me and a gift I cherish.

The most important thing I have learned thus far is to love myself, love others and never give up. I matter! You matter! Life is not easy but life is doable. Sometimes it's just plain hard, incredibly lonely and excruciatingly sad. Sometimes I have to stand alone but usually not for too long. Sometimes I have to face uncomfortable feelings to get to the happy ones. Sometimes I have to walk through fears to find my strength. Sometimes I have to cry and cry until the pain subsides. Sometimes I am blamed for things I didn't do, hated by people who don't know me or get me, or am humiliated by my own actions or those of others. Sometimes I'm heartbroken or broken down. As long as I never give up and find the truth, I have a fighting chance!

I am grateful for every moment I have and every moment I share with wonderful people. Thanks for taking this journey with me and may yours be all that you imagine it can! You are possible just as I'm possible! Say it to yourself over and over – I'M POSSIBLE, I'M POSSIBLE, I'M POSSIBLE – and you will be because you already are! BE TRUE TO YOURSELF AND ALWAYS BE YOU! You are enough! You are loved! You are powerful! You are amazing! You are wonderful! You are needed! You are valued! I say it and I believe it. Will you?

You can do anything that you want. That is the truth. What you have to overcome is doubt and fear. You have to be dedicated to being more and more courageous. Even when you are scared, alone and want to quit. Remind yourself over and over –

NOTHING IS IMPOSSIBLE BECAUSE I'M POSSIBLE!

Visualize your dreams daily. Get a journal and cover it with clippings from magazines that remind you of the accomplishments you want to make. Your dreams can and will come true if you do the work and stay true to yourself and your purpose.

If 50 years passed and your name came up in a history class, what would you want people to say about you and your contribution to the world?

Write down 2 people that you will share what you have learned.

1.

2.

Write down your goals for the next three years. You have to have a vision of what you want in life. It can always change, but let's start now.

1.

2.

3.

Each and every one of us is here for a Divine reason. Everything that happens in the physical happens in the spirit first. Lightness and darkness cannot survive in the same place. Be the Light and ask yourself – am I living as my greatest self? Am I trying as hard as I could? Am I giving up? What can I do to be my best?

I charge you to continue to move forward in your life and be determine to be the most excellent BIG YOU possible. You are filled with so much potential, everyday is a opportunity to take any challenge you face and let it motivate you into being your GREATEST! It may not be easy but It IS POSSIBLE! YOUR ARE A GREAT BIG PART OF THE WHOLE THAT MAKES LIFE.

GO AHEAD LITTLE ME
SHOW THE WORLD WHAT YOU GOT!

Made in the USA
Middletown, DE
06 July 2017